Field Notes for Extinction

Field Notes for Extinction

poems

Mark Caskie

GRAYSON BOOKS
West Hartford, Connecticut
graysonbooks.com

Field Notes for Extinction
Copyright © 2026 by Mark Caskie
Published by Grayson Books
West Hartford, Connecticut
ISBN: 979-8-9985883-5-8
Library of Congress Control Number: 2026933260

Book and Cover Design by Cindy Stewart
Cover Art by Austin Caskie
Author Photo by Dylan Caskie

for Patricia with love

Contents

ONE

Natural History

Forget the baleen, and its throat too narrow
to shove a fist through, its slick swell of back
festooned with sucker fish, barnacles,
streamers of seaweed hooked in the crook
of fins, its gentle nuzzles against the ship,
its plaintive, subsonic wail to its brothers—
believe the old tales of its merciless pursuit
of clippers, crashing through quiet hulls,
its angry eyes rimmed with red vengeance,
its love of human flesh, its greedy maw
swallowing you whole as you slide
down the soft, pink chute into its belly,
cluttered with the wreckage of history—
explorers' maps frayed and creased,
broken bifocals, a twisted bird cage,
a blue-and-gold epauletted uniform
still folded in a captain's chest,
the old galley table with its lamp,
the rusted harpoon pierced into its gut
half-floating in the swill at your feet—
recognize these things as yours,
you belong in this place, among your
broken artifacts, the spent days of
the voyage you captained. You would
cage 25 miles of birds, and
boil the flesh of whales to perfume
your bloodied fingers—go ahead, refine
the oil for your lamps, light the lantern,
it is better to see where you came from.

Black Snake

We stalked with long-handled shovels
the snake sulking away through the dandelions.
By the drainpipe, we severed the head
in brutal strokes, the tail writhing after.
The pattern that we had seen,
and the diamond-shaped head,
had been imaginary.
A black snake lay dead in the grass.
Too close to the house, you said, consoling.
We had to act fast, I said.
Flies settled iridescent on the parts.

The Fisherman's Map
—for Phil

Across the wall hangs North Central Pennsylvania
washed in a light willow-green on white paper,
as if painted on flanks of birch, though
closer inspection reveals the paper merely old,
the snakes and whirlpools' contour lines.
Still, it's a wilderness to contemplate
between fly ties, or late-night winters,
when the house crouches too close. Far away,
the precise graphs of roadbed gradients,
the tune of the mortgage pinging the roof,
for he knows in that green dome, fabulous
configuration of waters, thin hairline
blue moss cushion of creeks and rivers,
that there is a trout so wild, so
remote no fisherman could find it.
He imagines it visible in some sky pool,
its rose-stippled stomach, embered evening,
its yellow speckles, a cupful of stars—
there and not there below a tumbled
shelf of water, the sheer white jets
of some fall—the trout, unattainable.
Every cast he has ever laid
in the corner of a pool has been a failed
try at origins. Now nowhere,
far away from the jeep-trailed woods,
the fishermen's camps, the bushwhacked
briared paths, he dreams of it
in the somewhere of the denseness
of the map's correspondences, ideal
platonic realm of the irrational,
primitive maelstrom blueprinted
for consultation, tacked firmly
against the wall, surrounded by books,

computer screens, the civilized
geometry of doors, windows, vents.

Arctic Memoirs

—for Jim

He travels once again into the imaginary
circumference of the Arctic; with ice floes

the size of station wagons; and Spitzbergen,
a distant coast creviced by frost heaves

turned black with soil, like the plowed drifts
of parking lots. From his study, he hears

the furnace fire, could almost believe
his house ruddered; and he steering clear

of the driveway and bushes, the puzzle
of suburban streets, to surge across

cold spume the color of polar bears,
his split-level crashing through icebergs,

as if he could again hold binoculars
and see the brief revelation

of the Arctic summer, the resurrection
of uncharted waves, horizon-skimming sun.

Later, his tires trundled in chains,
he will inch his car over slick puddles,

packed snow, a mall trip for paper
and prescriptions—the dull routines

of his old age. And he thinks, if he could,
he would delay his arrival at final port,

its brightly painted houses, too like
a string of discount chains, though already,

his ship has left Spitzbergen in a fog,
and returned as far as Bear Island.

This time the rock is invisible—
no sun flashes through the cliff,

the wink of the thunder god, as it did
on his outward voyage. But even

this bunk-ridden stint, in which he holes
up from the cold to complete calculations

for airstrips, is better than what follows—
the ice that shears the rudder, the long

tow toward port, the inconclusive
burial of his report in some Pentagon

archive. For now, his computer screen glows
the color of pack ice. He stubs a cigarette

butt against a windowpane, remembers
a Norwegian he once saw spear a seal.

Canoe Song

—for Patricia

Without a paddle stroke, the wind
drives me up lake, miraculously
between the shoals of reeds.
I would wish you here
to see the black-crested kingfisher
drop out of the sky to rise
with a minnow, shiny and flapping,
in its dagger beak, or
perhaps, more to your liking,
the mother mallard, her incredible
brood of twelve ducklings, incredibly
lining up for inspection.
I could go on—
there's the blue heron,
who imagines himself invisible
behind his cloak of reeds,
his long, crooked neck,
sticking a good two feet higher.
Of course, you've seen these things.
Together, we've remarked on
the bird-like water arums, the fleshy,
yellow pistils of those lilies.
Back at the cabin, you're sketching
one in watercolor, worrying
over the brilliant inner secret
of this flower, which no
hue seems to match.
I hope you're drinking a cup
of coffee, playing some jazz—
Charlie Parker always makes
for looser brushwork.
As for me, I've drifted
as far as the river, while I've

been writing this poem, and have
come to rest in the intense green
reeds that gather at its mouth.

Aunt Eva and Aunt Annie, 1915

With sixteen stippled trout strung
across a plank, you had outdone
all the men. It had made little difference
to your father since he had wanted
boys. Still, there were the young men,
and so before you allowed them
to take a photograph of your
catch, you changed into long white
dresses, with loose-fitting blouses
and bows at the neckline.
In the picture, you have drawn
your arms quietly behind you.
Aunt Eva, you didn't even look
at the camera, as if embarrassed
by your beauty, or believing
a gentleman caller would
tease you over this photograph.
Aunt Annie, you look directly out,
satiric, as if you could chock
any evening full of laughs.
What response did you make
to the jokes of men, over
the prodigious bit of luck
that could bring such a catch?

If only they had seen you casting
your lines along the sunken logs,
or the way you baited your hooks without
flinching, the way you scrubbed the blood
off your hands before returning.

Cousin Elliot Brockton, 1956

You're playing chess
and smoking the pipe that will kill you.
It's full of J. Wright tobacco,
your favorite, the paisley tin
poking out of your pocket.
This passion for chess,
in the last years of your life
so incongruent with the rest of it,
working in steel mills, drinking
Genesee with buddies. Orphaned young,
you were a rough one, all right,
but kind too. As you got older,
you must have realized
those photos in the family cottage,
those genteel Victorians displaying
catches of fish in full suit and tie,
were your grandparents and great-grandparents.
Professor types, you used to call them,
though you spent less and less
time in the boat and more
with your plastic chess pieces,
studying the moves of the masters
from a book as if you could
conjure the past you never had.
Anyway, that's how I remember you.
Your fishing tackle dusty
on the shelf, as you stoked
your pipe, and ruminated
over strategies to capture
an opposing king.

Gregory Brockton, 1932

Depression-tough, you held on to your
job at the mill despite the long
hours, the low wages, the shanty
on the outskirts of Milton.
Your whitewalled Model-T
just edges into the picture,
the one you kept running
by scouring junkyards
and once even stripping
the wiring out of the wall
of your shack. In the foreground,
you squat, right arm around
your collie, Buster, who looks
skittishly at the camera,
as if he was used to having
stones thrown at him before
you took him in. In your
left hand, a thin white
cigarette held scoop fashion,
put out just long enough
for your brother to take
the picture he insisted
on taking on his visit
up from Pennsylvania.
You're quite serious in this photo,
a man who is willing to stay
in one place and to work
for his wages.

There is another picture,
Buster sits on the hood
of your Model-T, his tongue out, ears
perked, eager for one of the rides
you used to take him on,

the two of you, driving country lanes,
spinning your dust into oblivion.

Rain and Smoke

She sat on the porch swing, watching.
First the downspouts and as the intensity increased,
curtains of water along the front
overspilling the gutters.
The downspouts were almost bursting,
thick, arm-size chutes of water, bubbled and milky,
hit the concrete drainboards and spewed across the grass
beneath the gold dust and azalea bushes,
combing the grass into individual blades.
It reminded her of a certain waterfall
she had walked behind. She remembered
how once as a girl
her family had driven in a rainstorm like this one
up on the parkway,
when a storm squall had
dropped over the mountain.
Her father pulled over at the scenic view
where there was no view,
a cloud with no clear beginning or ending.
The rain thumped against the steaming hood.
Her father tried to tune the radio,
the dial lighted like lightning in a bottle.
He took off his hat, rubbed his hands
through his hair—
was it from weariness or uneasiness?
A gesture she had seen before.
The smell of his leather hat, the stale smell of cigarettes
mingled in the moist air.
The smoke trailed feebly out
his small triangular window.
Then,
the sky cleared,
the valley loomed up from underneath,
Distance brought close, she could see cows
huddled together beneath trees.

Life and death,
she thought sitting on her porch all alone,
are like rain and smoke.
Now, seeing farther than she had wanted to see.

Over Waves and Troughs

We hunch around the oil lantern,
listening to the broad oar strokes
in the cadence of stories
everyone has to tell: dirty-gray

clouds throwing lightning
and the tangles of lime-green
seaweed on legs and arms
pulling us down like nets.

We discuss strategies, ways
to swim out of the thrall of
rip currents, the use of the dead
man's float to preserve life.

The room floats in the warm
flicker of light, the evening
drifts on, its currents carry us
slowly, shifting our perspectives

as our shadows group tightly
as survivors in a raft.
Who was this boy who drowned?
Each of us saw him, his black

flattop and swimming trunks,
athletic build, so strong and light
he should have been carried over
the waves like a porpoise.

Each of us has feared the unexpected
touch of his clammy, rigid hand
as we swim. His body never
found, no proof he ever existed.

Outside, the tide rises, the wind
shakes our cozy cottage. We have
all had a dream with towering
waves and malicious caps,

and clouds, and a shore no one
would wish to ever reach, in which
the boy in black floats near, nearer,
no longer looking innocent,

but reaching for us with the slow,
pulsing movements of a jellyfish.
Slowly, we guide our conversation
out of these waters. No one is

willing to say the truth about the boy,
or the uninviting shore in the dream.
We clutch the table tighter
as it spins over waves and troughs.

TWO

Nurse

A child homesick and alone in a hospital,
I wondered what the nurse's words meant.
She had cried out after she had drawn
the plunger, nearly injected
me with air. I searched her eyes, face—
found no answer, saw her trembling hands.
Then, her silence as she straightened,
patted my shoulder, as if to say,
dear boy, this must be *our* little secret.

Drunk

When the man who had whistled
the theme song of one of America's favorite
TV shows performed on our school stage,
no one was close enough to smell his breath.
But there were other signs—slurred speech,

the way he held the microphone stand
as if staying upright against terrible winds.
*I can whistle melody and harmony
at the same time,* he boasted.
But his whistling proved shrill, his remarks

incoherent. Later, back in the classroom,
our teacher's eyes narrowed—
What did you think of him? she asked.
At first no one said a word.
Then, without looking up, a classmate

asked *Was he drunk?* The teacher
didn't respond, but the boy—
who was frequently absent, sometimes
appearing with mysterious bruises—
must've already known the answer.

Objet d'Art

Disheveled and sweaty from the bus
ride ruckus, crazed museum wanderings

of my boy tribe, I pressed close to the glass case
to see the tiny city of gold—pitched bridges,

sumptuous galleries, ornate fountains, windows
jeweled with rubies. Awestruck, I wondered,

how people could survive in that place—
even then, sensing the untidiness

of human wants, the unevenness of love.
How could we grow old in that citadel

that allowed for no imperfections?

Garden Apartments

Every spring, the cherry tree in the courtyard
blossomed white as a snow princess' gown.
Upstairs, a mezzo-soprano practiced arias,
and in a building across the way,
a violinist tuned his instrument with a frown,
then launched into a concerto—or two.
We opened the window the better to hear
and take in the fragrant spring air.

Rumor was the musicians had never met,
though we could picture no surer romance
than one between soloist and diva.
Young, we imagined our future a bright,
unbroken line. Later razed, the apartments
have left no trace of grace or innocence.

Showering in the Dark

The wafting steam clouds
the glass panes,
muting the alley light.
I stand naked,
groping for the soap
in its dish. Darkly,
the day washes off,
I move in a dream
of my own body, glad
to only half-see the hints
of age: the gray chest hairs,
the slackened muscles.
My muscles flex to touch
where we only touch
to clean: armpits, back,
even between toes,
like an Egyptian woman,
wrapping the pharaoh's feet
in balms of myrrh, or
the care of a Roman wife
whose husband has
returned from a long march,
and who prepares
to leave again tomorrow.

Jacket

For months after my father died,
my mother wore his favorite jacket,
her small frame engulfed by its size.
Then, one day, the jacket was gone.
I guessed she'd donated it
to Goodwill. I scoured
the city from my car window
for the stranger who was wearing it—
gray mohair, red and white stripes
across the chest. Did I feel
some need to reclaim the jacket?
I never saw it again. I never
asked why it had disappeared.

Winter Rations

In that northern city, where the snow fell
and cold seeped a hand's-width past the pane,
you lay in your sick bed, stroke-stricken, mute.
I pulled up Google Earth, turned the screen
toward you, inched along rural roads
leading to your long-ago home—
up Clearview, past horse pastures,
a medley of red, pink, white, lavender azaleas,
stony-faced Panther Mountain looming
but still distant, onto Little Texas, past
the linear meadow of the waterline
into the hairpin curve, out again, up
the hill past the neighbor's, the creek,
at last arriving at your garden, driveway
leading off into woods. The garden
caught in a perpetual spring—
pea blossoms on the trellis, strawberries
beginning to turn red and lush.
Pleased with my work, the unexpected
freshness of the garden, its promise of bounty,
I turned to look at your face, expectant.
You're home, I said, and then said it again.
You might have mumbled the word *amazing*.
I couldn't be sure. Was it just wishful thinking?
Outside, the snow swirled. Hungry deer
foraged on bitter brush in the distance.

Drawing Hands

I draw gestures from fists to open palms,
cupped hands and fingers spread wide

until my drawings are looped together,
intersected, smudged by the pull of

my hand across the paper until nothing
human is left. Wingbeats swirl

across the page, deer lift their hooves
in flight before an unseen gun.

And I draw still more, crowding in spaces,
barbing existing lines until

I see only the hoof-beaten briars,
the ribbed cloud cover of empty skies—

what remains here is absence. Far away
from my hand, my other

hand has been busy making my life,
magnifying flaws, splotches, distorting

intentions by the piling on of hands.
I want new paper, a sharp pencil,

a clean eraser, time to untangle
every gesture, to redraw

the lines of my palm, to learn
my every fist, extended hand.

Leaf

If I am the crinkled brown leaf
that falls dizzy with age,
shrivels in the grass where rain weakens
me into a hatchwork of
windows,
and I am gathered
into a sheet, and tossed into a ditch,
the fire curling me, snapping my
spine as I hiss,
then I will flee as smoke
these tangled snares of limbs.

On the Metro

"Just as any of you is one of a living crowd, I was one of a crowd."
—Walt Whitman

Bodies press against strangers
on the evening subway commute.
Faces stare at the ceiling, worn orange
carpet with muddy shoe tracks
to preserve our pretend privacy.
The train heads toward the Potomac.

The tracks clack, high-pitched
wails in the curves at first, then
we slow, stop at what seems
the lowest point under the river.
Conductor says, *We have a delay, folks,*
should be only a few minutes.

I wish I could pull a book
out of my pack, so I could distract
myself, but there's no room
to move. Like Whitman, I'm one
of the crowd but claustrophobic.

I crane my neck to read the only ad
I can see—a pregnancy helpline
for teenagers, study passengers' hands
that clutch metal poles—wrinkled or young,
rings on fingers, watches on wrists—

but my thoughts soon rise above
my surroundings. First, the ceiling
holding back all that water, then the mud
of the riverbed, cluttered with rotting
boat boards, dilapidated piers,

bones, plastic. Catfish probe
the bottom debris, fish schools rocket
through open water. On the surface,
scullers glide on a glittering day,
seagulls appear as white banners

in the sky. (I lose sight of them
when they fly beneath the clouds.)
For a moment, I forget where I am, until
a slow train arrives on the other track
in the tunnel. I peer through

the reflections of those packed in my train,
apparitions in the glass, at the throng
of strangers going in the opposite direction—
my envy borders on hate as they go by,
oblivious to us, eyes only for themselves.

THREE

Japanese Print

In the Japanese print on my wall
the waves are silver-gray
with strong peaks, the white froth
sneers at the peasant
fisherman in his shallow-drafted
boat. The orange-red fish who leap
about the boat are each half
as big as the man. They have
beaten the water into its fury
with their tails—for revenge?
Or is it just a kind of mischief?
In the man's tired face,
I see the long hours spent
in the darkness, mending his nets
by feeble lantern-glow,
his long fingers searching
out the tears, thread-bare points,
and tangles from which his meager
livelihood might escape. Only this,
a sudden leadening of the skies
has caught him unprepared, as
it might any of us. Too late, though
he augured every sign and portent,
the haloed moons, the red skies
of evening and morning, the changes
in the color of the sea.

His Life as a Fish

They teased the small boy, said he was turning into a fish till he would crane his small hand behind his back to feel the fish scales, small sticky wedges like teeth that had failed to harden along the spine and the tiny wings of his shoulders. One said gills were beginning to edge in under his jawline too, and a spot on either cheek like the ones on the small fish they had been reeling in all day. Everyone knew, though, he had stood too close to his father when he was cleaning that catch of fish. They teased him for days. Nowhere in the cottage was there a mirror low enough that he could see it wasn't true. Within a week, he was refusing to wear his life jacket. His father whipped him, refused to let him in the water, though he would sneak out at night, stay down for minutes at a time, where his freckles grew iridescent, and no one could lay a hand on him. His eyes shifted wider until they reached the sides of his head. Then he disappeared, swimming in the swaying kelp, until his father jerked him out, his pursed mouth sucking for water, and he flapped furiously on the beach. When his father ripped the trebled hook out, it left a pair of gills. He tossed the boy into a bucket, but a wave toppled it, and he escaped, a flash of silver across the green surf.

The Sparrows in the Bush

Its rattle in the wind seems tame,
though its green specter-spikes of flame
hold a thorny intricacy
for red tails watching from the tree,
and the cat that lurks about its leaves
soon finds his probing paw can bleed.
In its fierce house the sparrows sing,
and hoard dry bits of grass and string,
and skirmish to stake community
upon this burning certainty,
the growth of summer may yet bring
a denser thicket to hide bare wings,
the helpless hatchlings that would quake
defenseless against a hawk or snake.

Winter Scene

The cardinals
gather the Samaritan's
sunflower seeds
about the three
marble ladies
who hoist the frozen
birdbath filled
with snow.
These birds aren't
the red berries
of winter skies
or the wine-colored
disciples of St.
Francis.
Glinty-eyed,
they tweak with fury,
flick tails
aggressively.
So hungry
they fight, scatter
feathers for a single,
uneaten seed.

Pigeons

I had always thought of them as comic relief—
denizens of building ledges, panhandlers of city parks.
But today, pigeons soar above the river beneath
bridge arches, wingbeats as steady as scullers' oars,
flashing black bars with every stroke.
All afternoon, I watch their acrobatics,
imagine them on some untamed and rocky coast.
These same clouds racing high above cliffs.

Field Notes for Extinction

Species: Ivory-billed woodpecker

Date: 1.13.2025; temp: 28° F; weather: clear skies, light wind

Photos: None

Location: 100 miles from somewhere

Observations: Large woodpecker with crest, heavy bill, and white-and-black plumage drumming on large dead tree, sometimes dislodging bark

Impressions: Drumming sounds like thunder. Crest like a giant red flame. Bill the color of delicate scrimshaw.

Habitat: Old-growth forests, dreams

Status: Marginal or extinct

Conservation: Mourn the ivory billed when you enter the woods by repeating its nasal song, *kent kent, kent kent, kent kent*. Listen to the silence that follows.

Prairie Park

What I know of the past
In history books, photos of men
stoop beside severed buffalo heads,
swagger atop heaps of buffalo bones.
Stories of men shooting buffalo
from passing trains for sport.

What I know of the present
Today, along the park road,
cars splay at angles; people snap
photos, hoard trophy shots.
The buffalo arranging
and rearranging, a shifting tableau—

one rolls in the red clay, dust rising;
a cow suckles her calf; others graze,
heads bowed in the tall, blonde grass.
All calm, until a reckless man
with a camera gets too close.
A bull charges, relentless

as a locomotive, steam rising
from wet nostrils. He chases the man
to his car. The bull rams it twice.
The man loses his camera. I hit
my car horn—is it to scare the buffalo
or to celebrate its small victory?

Octopus Corpse

No bigger than my hand, burnt umber
with black freckles, organs appearing as dark

shadows beneath the skin, six gelatinous
tentacles—the other two torn off

by some carnivore. The corpse
reminds me of aliens in sci-fi films,

elongated limbs, oversized
craniums—a sure sign of

extraterrestrial intelligence.
The octopus may embody the other,

but what I'm curious about is the animal
I cradle in my palm, not human constructs.

I marvel at a body so flexible it could
swim through a sunken ship's

tiniest keyhole. When alive, chromatophores
pulsed vermillion, yellow ocher, carmine,

magenta, midnight black to hide
from predators—yet nothing could help

it evade death when the time came.
We have *that* in common.

Wild Clays of Montgomery County

Unprocessed, wood fired in a kiln, the wild
clays in the exhibit come in earthy colors—
charcoal, butterscotch, taupe with blue-gray.
Unformed by human hands, these chunks
of earth reveal more about this place
than the finished products on sale
in the gallery—the same way uncut minerals
expose more than faceted, polished stones.
These wild clays root me in this terrain of pines,
forgotten fields, dry ridges, sluggish creeks,
hard-scrabble lives eked out on poor soils.

Identifying Pines

Sometimes, I know the pine
from a single feature—broad plates
of shortleafs, the needles of longleafs.

Other times, I count needles in a bundle,
make measurements, assess needle color,
then bark and cones—
are they grayish or reddish-brown?

The field guide says this pine lives
less than a human lifetime,
while the one next to it lives for centuries,
longer than eight human generations.

The first step is always to learn the names.

The deciduous trees dominate the woods
in fall with outsized personalities,
but in winter, after colors retreat,
pines catch the eye—
straight trunks as sure as just-hewn ship masts,
green needles brushing against a cold blue sky.

FOUR

Cairns

1
In Scotland,
I found them in fog, and deeper
into a cloud bank they led.
Old lichen covered piles
all shaggy bearded, squatting
prehistoric men turned to
cold, mute stone. I
stumbled on sheared shards,
and though I watched,
not once did they breathe. Those
dark silhouettes on the hillside.

2
You reached the top first, and when
I caught up
I found the stones in your hands.
The pile was as big as a car.
Hikers milled about drinking water,
eating gorp,
their bright jackets and packs
hurt my eyes.
I added my rocks as well,
some had been spray-painted.
I thought of hands against stone,
how we all come to hate scree.

3
The magazine shows
them like giants,
signposts for Inuits,
bleak and treeless land.

4

If Snyder is right, then words
are also stones.
I think of galleries full
of minerals encased in glass,
the beveled, purple interiors
of geodes,
chalky cliffsides of sulfur,
of bat-dark phosphorescence.
Dictionaries,
poems piled together into books.

5

Back in the Depression, the hobos would
leave small inconspicuous cairns
by roadsides, near houses where meals
could be had. My grandmother
made them stand on the porch,
eating cold chicken or a bowl of soup.
They always returned the plate,
inquired about work thereabouts.
In their eyes, the freights ran.
In their clothes, the alley smell of cities.
Cairns no higher than shoe tops
guided them from meal to meal.

Midwest

Horizons dissolve
as fog engulfs
farmhouses, barns, silos.
Clustered together
in snowy fields,
the buildings
loom like islands
in frozen seas.

Weeds

Bent spikes, brittle, blackish stems
coated in gauzy, gray cobwebs.

Seed pods busted open, matchhead-sized
seeds half-tumbled out.

Whirling wind takes them aloft,
suspended on silky parachutes.

Sweet Gum

Leaves like stars a child might make—
five-pointed, colored burnt orange,
scarlet, violet, drawn with a waxy crayon—
all on a single tree, bark
fissured, scaly as alligator skin.
Spiky, reddish-brown fruit
the nemesis of barefoot children.

Raccoon Pantoum

Firemen sometimes rescue cats stuck in trees,
but treed racoons must wait all day to escape,
while dogs run in endless circles, barking hoarsely,
until they grow bored and dream in fretful sleep.

But treed raccoons must wait all day to escape,
they watch among the branching pines
until they grow bored and dream in fretful sleep
of streams filled with fat and lazy fish.

They watch among the branching pines
the cats who dared to climb toward the sun,
of streams filled with fat and lazy fish,
they do not dream but fussily clean their paws.

The cats who dared to climb toward the sun
mew loudly for ladders and helping human hands,
they do not dream but fussily clean their paws
while dogs run in endless circles, barking hoarsely,

until they grow bored and dream in fretful sleep
of tiny human-like hands, the sudden strike of claw on nose.
Treed raccoons must wait all day to escape,
but firemen sometimes rescue cats stuck in trees.

The Fish

If we caught the fish, we'd put them back because we knew there were only a few, and besides they were too small to eat, though even in our tiny fishing hole we rumored a large catfish lived, who would pull any boy in, who stuck his leg in too far. We'd rig up our sticks with a nail and string, hook the worms and lower our lines into the slow, counterclockwise spin of the foam and water, tea-colored from the leaf muck that rocked on the bottom. Nearby, a stump fallen sideways formed the wash, its roots corkscrewing in every direction like Medusa's snakes. The small fish we'd catch were pale and white, missing their protective layer of scales, albinos escaped from a nearby cave. I remember clutching those limp bodies in my palm, studying them before I withdrew the hook, threw them back; where, without so much as a flap of their tails, they'd disappear into the depths. Now, I think of those fish, poor, starving creek fish, with scarcely enough to live. The small, pink scars in their mouths and gills from hooks meant to keep a small boy happy, or perhaps to keep some creek fish alive.

At the Nature Center

The copperhead in the display case
struck its meal with outstretched fangs,
injected toxins, then curled up
waiting for the mouse to die,
raw wounds on the mouse's neck

and shoulder. The mouse raced
to the back of the case, then raced
back by the snake before falling
into the water dish. Paws paddling
for a long time—to the point

or past the point of exhaustion.
When the mouse found the rim
at last, it went to the far corner.
The mouse seemed to grow sleepy.
Balance off, it tipped to one side.

The snake slithered over to check
on its meal—the mouse came over
to meet the snake, as if it knew how
this would end. I'll spare you the rest.
You can imagine it, if you wish to.

***

No doubt, I've already given you
too much detail. *What is the point,*
you may ask, *of a mouse's death?*
I ask in return, *Is your heart racing?*
Is your body growing heavy?

I wrote this poem to assuage
a troubling memory. Now, it's your
memory too. *Little mouse, shake*
the poison if you can.

Specter Fish

"I do not believe in ghosts. I believe in ghost stories."
—*John Robert Colombo*

Somewhere in the dark inlet
it lurks, gliding as if sustained

by the motion of wings
while waders pull against my movements

like anchors. I fasten my flashlight beam,
its penetrating eye, past teeming

foam, beyond the mottled surfaces.
I seek the dark hiding spots, shadows

darting in the flashlight beam
but the swirling sand chokes

my clear remembrance of its habits,
tell-tale clues of where

it lies, alive but half-buried,
its skin freckled and shaded

to elude the hunter.
Condensation seeps against

my skin, currents tug
fiercely against my legs.

Encased in my waders, my pliable shell,
so like a moveable tomb or a coat

of peat, I step along the limit
of the sandy bar, arms aching

from light and gig held
adrenalin-tight above the waves.

Suddenly, I see the double eye,
the red-rimmed double presence,

through the pulsing, pale surf.
I lunge at the specter fish.

Around my feet, sand explodes in a squall
of murk, I feel the wriggling flesh,

the convulsed heart, my tines driven
through the ribs and backbone.

Columns of blood rise
till I lift out the gig and find no sign,

only the clean tines glinting,
for the water refracts the aim.

What I hunt has slipped beyond
my thrust, beyond clear memory

toward some haunt in the bowl
of first creation, loose ganglia among

shipwrecks, mossy and barnacled,
of armadas lost in the whip-sting of storm.

Cacti

Cradled in their pots,
they seem to need only air and sunlight.
Flourishing best with negligence,
they're self-reliant to a fault,
they hoard water and protect it
with malicious barbs.

Olive and artichoke green
plant tissue, spiky stubble,
without blooms or fruit,
They seem too plain for comparisons,

Though people *might* be like cacti
with the virtues (or stupidity)
of self-reliance, or (for better or worse)
of an inwardly focused life.

But clumped together on my desk,
the thorny cacti are ornery,
resolute in their factual presence,
refusing metaphor with their prickly essence.

No ideas but in things, Williams insisted.
(Unless, of course, the things resisted.)

Language falters then fails.

I clear my desk clutter,
imagine a long road,
a radio that can find no signal,
a sunset in a still, stifling desert.
As I hurtle past in my car,
I see cacti silhouetted on a hill
Separate, far from any human needs.

Acknowledgments

I gratefully acknowledge the following journals for publishing these poems, sometimes in slightly different forms:

Connecticut River Review: "Natural History"

Flying South: "Aunt Eva and Aunt Annie, 1915," "Cousin Elliot Brockton, 1956," "Cairns," "Showering in the Dark"

Kakalak: "Winter Rations," "Over Waves and Troughs," "Nurse"

Pikeville Review: "Gregory Brockton, 1932"

South Coast Poetry Journal: "Black Snake"

Split Rock Review: "The Fisherman's Map"

Story South: "Canoe Song"

Zone 3: "Japanese Print"

About the Author

Mark Caskie was born in Richmond, Virginia, and earned his MFA at the University of North Carolina at Greensboro. He has published poetry in numerous literary journals including *Connecticut River Review*, *Story South*, and *Split Rock Review*. His poems often reflect his engagement with the natural world. He has two wonderful grown sons. *Field Notes for Extinction* is his debut collection.

www.ingramcontent.com/pod-product-compliance
Lightning Source LLC
Chambersburg PA
CBHW061359140726
47997CB00003B/1275